Harald Jes

The Terrarium

With full-color photographs
Illustrations by Johann Brandstetter

2 CONTENTS

TYPICAL TERRARIUM ANIMALS

- They are "living fossils" that exhibit exciting behavior.

- Many lizards are reminiscent of the dinosaurs of long ago.

- They live in desert, savanna, or tropical rain forest habitat.

- They make special adaptations to specific habitats.

- They shed their skin.

- They lay eggs or bear live young.

- They are active by day (diurnal), by night (nocturnal), or at twilight (crepuscular).

Naturally, only a few characteristics are shared by the approximately 800 species of tarantulas, 6,000 species of reptiles, and 3,000 species of amphibians found in the wild in all temperate, subtropical, and tropical zones around the globe.

For example, body temperature. Arachnids, amphibians, and reptiles are ectothermic (cold-blooded) animals in which the temperature of their blood is influenced by the temperature of their environment. This saves an enormous amount of energy! Since their entire life cycle is regulated by external factors, we must provide, monitor, and regulate conditions for terrarium animals much more closely than for warm-blooded animals.

Another characteristic they have in common: Tarantulas, amphibians, and reptiles shed their skin regularly. Rapidly growing young animals outgrow their external covering more quickly, and therefore they shed more frequently than older animals.

DECISION MAKING

1 While it's true that terrarium animals do not need to be petted, they do require proper care.

2 Terrarium animals will barely display any affection for you, but as "living fossils" they make up for this with their interesting behavior.

3 Most of the animals offered for sale come from tropical regions and require specific climate control of their terrarium. Technology makes it possible but has its price.

4 Even terrarium animals can get sick, then it may be necessary to visit a veterinarian, which can be expensive.

5 Since some people do not like to feed animals to other animals, you should be aware of this necessity before acquiring your pet—or choose plant-eating species.

Important Considerations

Before you make the decision to care for one—or even several—terrarium animals, you should be aware that you are assuming what could be years of responsibility for your pets. Many tarantulas and reptiles can live more than 20 years. Check local regulations to ensure that your pet is legal.

You should also be realistic about estimating the time required for regular care of your animals. It's true that terrarium animals do not need to be taken for walks, but your care does take time—about four hours a week per animal.

Will *your* tarantula or snake also be accepted by the rest of the family? You should not expect any family member who is afraid of spiders or snakes to put up with a housemate of this sort.

Terrarium animals—except for tarantulas (see Hair flicking, page 55)—do not cause allergies in humans. The transmission of salmonella can be prevented by simple hygienic measures.

ACQUISITION AND ACCLIMATION

Terrarium animals hold a special fascination for us, primarily because they are so fundamentally different from mammals. Lizards in particular call to mind the dinosaurs of long ago that still capture our imaginations.

Origins and History

Amphibians and reptiles: The earliest fossil skeleton of a caudate (tailed amphibian) dates from the period more than 350 million years ago; the fossils of the first anurans (tailless amphibian) are 150 million years old. Over 260 million years ago, the first reptiles appeared, and from these evolved the gigantic forms known as dinosaurs, which then died out again over 60 million years ago. Of these primitive ancestors, only chelonians (turtles and tortoises), crocodilians, and the tuatara have survived nearly unchanged. The ancestors of the approximately 3,000 amphibian and 6,000 reptilian species emerged over 100 million years ago in the Cretaceous Period. Today, their descendants live in the temperate climate zones and are especially numerous in the tropics.

Tarantulas: The first clues to fossil relatives of modern tarantulas were found in amber from the Middle Devonian of North America. That means that their primitive ancestors were also around nearly 350 million years ago. Today, approximately 800 species live in the tropical and subtropical regions of Asia, Europe, Africa, America, and Australia. In America they are found in the southwestern states, where they wander the desert at night. Since tarantulas have barely changed over the course of their evolution, they—like chelonians, crocodilians, and the tuatara—are correctly called living fossils.

Acquiring the Animals

In the interest of the animals, it makes the most sense if you look for domestic captive-bred animals. You can get terrarium animals in the pet store, at reptile and tarantula expos, or from a terrarium keeper and breeder. Captive-bred animals are also frequently offered for sale in specialized magazines and club news-letters (see Information, page 62). If you read odd combinations of numbers in these ads, for example, 1.3, 2.0, or 0.1, this means: one male, three females; two males, one female. Males are to the left of the period; females are to the right.

White's Tree Frog is a large, easily kept amphibian species.

Look Before You Buy

As with everything, the cost-benefit ratio should be right. High prices do not always guarantee first-rate terrarium animals. Allow yourself plenty of time to make your selection, and pay attention especially to the following:

Nutritional status: Ribs, backbone, and pelvic bones should not be too prominent. On the body, tail, and thighs, the skin should be only slightly wrinkled.

Eyes: They should not be sunken or lie too deep in the sockets, and healthy animals should react to disturbances, for example hand movements, with flight or defense.

✔ The skin over eyes and lids must be cleanly shed. One or perhaps several layers of old skin on the eyes can lead to blindness.

✔ Snakes with hazy white to light blue eyes are not sick, but rather, are in the process of shedding, during which any disturbance should be avoided.

Skin: It must be free of swellings, blisters, and open festering wounds, which can be due to metabolic disorders, fungal skin infections, or bacterial infections.

✔ Patches of unsloughed skin in snakes can be attributed to these diseases as well, but can also be due simply to insufficient humidity.

✔ In lizards, especially those with adhesive lamellae on the toes, such as geckos and anoles, check for proper shedding on the toes, since remnants of old skin can sometimes cause constrictions.

Shell: Only in very young turtles can the shell yield to a slight pressure of the fingers; in older ones, it must be hard and rigid.

Mouth: It must be closed. Sudden opening and closing, especially if there is also a discharge or bubbles around the nose and mouth, indicates a cold. Discharges in the mouth, on the other hand, suggest inflammation of the jaws, intestinal disorders, or respiratory problems (see Diseases, page 48). **Note:** If any of these signs are present, refrain from buying the animal. And remember that very probably, the other animals in a terrarium like this are also infected.

Ectoparasites: Be sure to check all animals in a terrarium; since where there is one tick or mite, there are certain to be more. A slight infestation is not especially troublesome, but there is still a need for immediate action (see Diseases, page 48).

The Giant Toad climbs inquisitively into the prepared quarantine terrarium after transport.

Note: You should carry out this kind of treatment in the quarantine terrarium.

Bite wounds, scars, broken-off tails: Recent or superficial injuries are not dangerous, but represent a decrease in value, and probably faulty care in the past.

Tarantulas: You are advised against spiders that have a whitish fungus or lumps on the body, that have pulled their legs up under their body, or show signs of desiccation in which the abdomen is wrinkled and clearly shorter than the cephalothorax. Missing appendages as well as injuries to the body and legs can also be serious; a "bald spot" on the abdomen is completely harmless. The spider has simply defended itself by hair flicking (see page 55) and brushed off the hairs; they will be back as good as new after the next molt.

Transporting the Animals

Reptiles are usually transported in a clean cloth bag, turtles or larger lizards in a box as well (see illustration, page 50).

Amphibians come in a plastic container filled with damp moss or sponge, aquatic amphibians in a plastic bag filled with water.

Tarantulas are safely transported in a covered deli cup, which is lined with damp paper for longer trips.

Protection from Cold

In chilly weather, you can carry small packages under your jacket; larger containers are transported in a Styrofoam box. In addition, for long distances, you'll need to warm up this box to 80°F (27°C) with a hot water bottle or with heat packs from the pet store.

Note: Never transport the animal in an open basket, in your hand, or on a leash. Aside from getting cold, it could escape and give unsuspecting passersby a severe shock.

TIP

Alone or in a Community?

While tarantulas are acknowledged loners, most amphibians and reptiles are social creatures. All the species mentioned are suitable for housing in a community. In nature, number increases safety; for example, many eyes spot a (hungry) enemy more quickly. A community terrarium promotes interaction among the terrarium animals, much as they do in nature. Number and size of the pets must be taken into account when determining the space. However, not every community can be expanded at will, because long-term occupants of the terrarium can make life difficult for the newcomers. If you want to keep more than one species in a terrarium, make sure that not only are they compatible, but, above all, that they come from the same climate.

Acclimation

Until the animal is free of parasites, healthy, and eating regularly, it should be isolated in a quarantine terrarium to get acclimated. Only here do you have the opportunity to observe behavior, state of health, food intake, and digestion of the animal (see Preventive Measures, page 48).

Crevice Spiny Lizards are diurnal reptiles and occupy hot dry habitats.

Furthermore, only in quarantine is it possible to take fecal samples selectively, which is important for evaluating the state of health. **Note:** Aquatic amphibians do not need to be quarantined if they are not to be integrated into an existing community. Captive-bred animals from an old and parasite-free population do not need to be quarantined.

The Quarantine Terrarium

A used aquarium, equipped with a screen cover, makes a good quarantine terrarium. Since it is only temporary housing, half of the space requirement given in the individual animal descriptions is sufficient (descriptions of popular terrarium animals begin on page 14). **Note:** Lighting and heating are necessary; side ventilation is a conditional requirement.

The setup can be spartan but must be hygienic, practical to manage, and suitable for the purpose (see illustration, page 10). On the cage bottom put a plastic turf terrarium liner, 5 to 10 mm thick, which is easy to clean and when suitably moistened, also provides the necessary humidity. In addition, many animals like to hide under it.
Note: For occupants of drier habitats, paper towels are also a suitable substrate material.

A water dish for drinking or bathing must be available. But never fill this too full, because water spills will be absorbed only to a certain extent by the substrate.

Climbing facilities for the animals are provided by branches, a tree limb, or an egg carton placed on its end, which can be thrown away when it gets dirty.

Hiding places can be made using terra-cotta pipes, bark, or the above-mentioned egg cartons.

Note: If the newcomers are especially shy and nervous, covering the cage with paper or towels is recommended; this is removed piece by piece after a few days in order to acclimate the animals gradually.

Care in the Quarantine Terrarium

The animal should really remain undisturbed as much as possible; therefore, only carry out the most necessary tasks such as:

✔ Changing the water in the drinking and bathing dishes, moistening the terrarium liner.

✔ Removing feces, if necessary changing paper or liner. Evaluate feces, but above all send it away at intervals for analysis (see Diseases, page 48).

✔ Feeding. The animal will not eat at first, and it should not worry you initially if, for example, it takes turtles or insectivorous lizards one week and snakes five or more weeks after arrival before they start eating again.

✔ When feeding for the first time, do not startle the animal. Leaves and fruits or live crickets or prekilled prey animals are simply placed in the cage.

✔ Do not move the animal to force its food, but rather allow it to settle down in the acclimation period.

Checklist
Things to Note When Buying

1 Before buying, research your choice so that you can select the right animals.

2 Do not be tempted to make impulse purchases; that can be expensive because of insufficient preparation.

3 Prepare the quarantine terrarium in advance so that the animals' stay in the transport container is as brief as possible.

4 The dealer's terrarium should be well cared for, the surrounding area should be neat. If the facilities are not clearly visible, the animals could be poorly maintained.

5 A good dealer will give you detailed advice. If his recommendations do not agree with the information you have already gathered, skepticism is in order.

6 The animals must be in good condition (see page 10). Healthy animals react to disturbances with flight or defense; therefore, only select them during their period of activity.

Popular Terrarium Animals

In this guide, only amphibians, reptiles, and tarantulas suitable for care in a beginner's terrarium have been selected. Animals with interesting behavior from various habitats are presented, especially those that have proven relatively easy to breed in captivity. This includes the possibility of breeding in the terrarium as well as propagation on farms in the countries of origin, since animals born in captivity do not have to be taken from their natural habitats.

Protection status: If you purchase a protected animal species (see Tip, page 23), you may someday need to provide proof of legal ownership. In the United States, CITES (Convention on International Trade in Endangered Species) is not particularly relevant. It is the Endangered Species Act that you must check. Obtain a receipt listing the scientific name from the dealer. Trade or barter in species that are designated as federally endangered is illegal.

Size of the animals: The average sizes of fully grown adult animals are given. The snout-vent length, from the tip of the snout to the cloaca, is important because of the considerable tail length of many lizards. For tarantulas, the body length of sexually mature females, which generally grow to be larger than the males, is given without appendages.

Behavior: Active during the day (diurnal), at night (nocturnal), or at dusk and/or dawn (crepuscular).

Terrarium size: The terrarium dimensions recommended in the descriptions give width × depth × height (see Tip, page 15).

Feeding recommendations: The information applies to half-grown and fully grown specimens; young animals must be fed more frequently.

Axolotl

Ambystoma mexicanum (see Photo, page 17)
Total length: 10 inches (25 cm).
Habitat: Mexico, heavily vegetated waters at high altitudes.
Behavior: Diurnal, crepuscular, and nocturnal.
Housing: Aquaterrarium, also without land area,

White's Tree Frog lives on branches and foliage in the tropical rain forest.

30 × 16 × 16 inches (75 × 40 × 40 cm).
Decoration: Bogwood, emergent and
submergent aquatic and climbing plants.
Temperature: 65 to 77°F (18–25°C).
Feeding: Three times a week (babies daily): daphnia, mosquito larvae, earthworms, chopped fish.
Similar to care for: **African Clawed Frog**
Xenopus laevis (see page 17), 4 inches (11 cm),
tropical Africa.

White-lipped Tree Frog

Litoria infrafrenata (see photo, page 16)
Total length: 3 inches (8 cm).
Habitat: New Guinea, Australia, tropical rain
forest, near bodies of water.
Behavior: Nocturnal and crepuscular.
Housing: Aquaterrarium 16 × 16 × 26 inches
(40 × 40 × 65 cm), about 2/3 land area,
water depth 4 to 8 inches (10–20 cm).
Decoration: Branches, plants with large, sturdy
leaves.
Temperature: Daytime 77 to 83°F (25–28°C), 68
to 77°F (20–25°C) at night.
Humidity: 75 to 95 percent.
Feeding: Twice a week (tadpoles daily): large
insects, newborn mice.
Special note: Do not keep together with small
frogs: predator!
Similar to care for: **White's Tree Frog** *Litoria
caerulea* (see page 8), 3 inches (8 cm),
Australia, New Guinea.

Oriental Fire-bellied Toad

Bombina orientalis (see photo, page 16)
Total length: 2 inches (5 cm).
Habitat: Eastern Asia, heavily vegetated waters
with weedy banks.
Behavior: Diurnal and crepuscular, social, takes
refuge in the water.
Housing: Aquaterrarium 20 × 8 inches (50 ×
20 × 20 cm) with island, water depth 4 inches
(10 cm).

TIP

Terrarium Size

The terrarium sizes presented in the
descriptions are based on housing
guidelines for reptiles. The sizes stated
apply for the body measurements of fully
grown animals given in the guide, but
not for rarely attained maximum sizes.

The basis for calculation is the total
length of amphibians and snakes, the
head-body length of lizards, the shell
length of turtles, and the body length of
tarantulas. The dimensions apply for
occupancy by two specimens. For each
additional animal, at least 20 percent of
the volume must be added on. If the
animals are only half as large, then divide
the measurements in half accordingly.
The sizes given are based on standard
terrarium measurements—but larger
never hurts!

Decoration: Moss-covered rocks or wood as an
island, emergent and submergent aquatic and
climbing plants.
Temperature: Daytime 68 to 77°F (20–25°C), 65
to 68°F (18–20°C) at night, in the winter up to
5°C lower.
Humidity: 70 to 90 percent.
Feeding: Twice a week (tadpoles daily): insects,
meadow plankton, small earthworms; at lower
temperatures significantly less is eaten.
Similar to care for: **Tiger Salamander**
Ambystoma tigrinum (see page 17), 10 inches
(25 cm), North America.

PORTRAITS:
AMPHIBIANS

Amphibians include caudates (tailed amphibians) like the Axolotl, and anurans (tailless amphibians) like the Giant Toad. They usually have four fingers on the front legs, five toes on the rear legs, the skin is glandular, moist, and does not have horny scales.

Photo right: White-lipped Tree Frogs like caging that is a bit moister than the caging of White's Tree Frogs.

Photo left: The Oriental Fire-bellied Toad spends a lot of time in the water.

Photo above: Typical of the Giant Toad are its large parotid glands.

The Ornate Horned Frog is a voracious predator.

Photo above: Although the African Clawed Frog breathes using lungs, it never leaves the water.

Photo above: The terrarium of the heavy White's Tree Frog needs sturdy plants.

Photo right: Tiger Salamanders like to stay on the damp substrate.

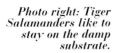

Photo below: The Moroccan Toad from North Africa is a very lively anuran.

The Axolotl has external gills throughout its life.

Giant Toad

Bufo marinus (see photo, page 16)
<u>Total length:</u> 6 inches (15 cm).
<u>Habitat:</u> Widely distributed throughout the tropics, tropical rain forest, cultivated areas such as sugarcane plantations; lives on the ground near water.
<u>Behavior:</u> Nocturnal and crepuscular.
<u>Housing:</u> Aquaterrarium 49 × 24 × 24 inches (120 × 60 × 60 cm), about 2/3 land area, water depth about 4 inches (10 cm).
<u>Decoration:</u> Epiphyte branches, climbing plants, but they must be unreachable or they will be destroyed.
<u>Temperature:</u> 77°F (25°C).
<u>Humidity:</u> 75 to 95 percent.
<u>Feeding:</u> Once or twice a week (tadpoles daily): insects, earthworms, occasional newborn mice.
<u>Special note:</u> Keep only with animals of a larger size, predator!
<u>Similar to care for:</u> **Moroccan Toad** *Bufo mauretanicus* (see page 17), 4 inches (10 cm), North Africa, lively anuran. **Ornate Horned Frog** *Ceratophrys ornata* (see page 16), 4 inches (10 cm), tropical South America, diurnal.

Red-bellied Side-necked Turtle

Emydura subglobosa (see photo, page 21)
<u>Shell length:</u> 6 inches (15 cm).
<u>Habitat:</u> New Guinea, water, stream banks.
<u>Behavior:</u> Diurnal, social, likes to swim.
<u>Housing:</u> Aquaterrarium

39 × 16 × 20 inches (100 × 40 × 50 cm), with hot spot for basking.
<u>Decoration:</u> Island, better yet, wood jutting up out of the water, with basking area.
Important Note: Plants climbing from above into the terrarium must remain out of reach of the animals, since there is a danger of escape.
<u>Temperature:</u> 77°F (25°C), basking area up to 95°F (35°C), UV light.
<u>Humidity:</u> 70 to 90 percent.
<u>Feeding:</u> Three times a week: daphnia, mosquito larvae, freshwater shrimp, chopped fish, earthworms, also vegetarian food.
<u>Similar to care for:</u> **New Guinea Snake-necked Turtle** *Chelodina novaeguineae* (see page 21), 8 inches (20 cm), New Guinea.

Leopard Gecko

Eublepharis macularius (see photo, page 20)
<u>Total length:</u> 8 inches (20 cm), head-body length: 5 inches (12 cm).
<u>Habitat:</u> Asia Minor, northwestern India, dry regions; seeks out cooler damp cavities during the day.
<u>Behavior:</u> Nocturnal and crepuscular, terrestrial.
<u>Housing:</u> Desert terrarium 16 × 12 × 12 inches (40 × 30 × 30 cm).
<u>Decoration:</u> Rockwork, sand, rounded stones with damp hiding places, xerophytic grasses.
<u>Temperature:</u> Daytime 86°F (30°C), 68°F (20°C) at night, during the rest period from November

Leopard Gecko—a gecko without adhesive lamellae on the fingers and toes.

to February constantly about 68°F (20°C).
Humidity: 50 to 70 percent.
Feeding: Three times a week: insects, newborn mice.
Special note: Water droplets are licked off the decorations; mist once a day.
Similar to care for: **African Five-lined Skink** *Mabuya quinquetaeniata* (see page 40), 10 inches (25 cm), head-body length 3.5 inches (9 cm), Central Africa, savannah, thornbush steppe.

Crevice Spiny Lizard
Sceloporus poinsetti (see photo, page 20)
Total length: 10 inches (26 cm), head-body length: 5 inches (12 cm).
Habitat: Southwestern North America, mountains up to 8,200 feet (2,500 m), hot dry rocky hillsides.
Behavior: Diurnal, terrestrial, social.
Housing: Desert terrarium 20 × 20 × 20 inches (50 × 50 × 50 cm).
Decoration: Rockwork, gravel, xerophytic shrubs.
Temperature: Daytime up to 104°F (40°C) in spots, but the animals must be able to move into cooler zones, 59°F (15°C) at night, during the rest period from November to February constantly 59 to 68°C (15–20°C), basking areas, UV light.

The African Five-lined Skink can be housed with the Leopard Gecko.

Humidity: 50 to 70 percent.
Feeding: Three times a week: insects, occasional newborn mice, also leaves and flowers.
Special note: Water droplets are licked up, mist once a day, viviparous.
Similar to care for: **Bearded Dragon** *Pogona vitticeps*, (see page 20), 20 inches (50 cm), head-body length 9 inches (22 cm), Australia, scrub, savannah forest.

Striped Basilisk
Basiliscus vittatus (see photo, page 20)
Total length: 30 inches (75 cm), head-body length: 8 inches (20 cm).
Habitat: Central America, tropical rain forest, always near water.
Behavior: Diurnal, arboreal, shy and nervous, social, likes to swim.

PORTRAITS: REPTILES

Reptiles include turtles, lizards, and snakes. They often have five fingers, five toes, and dry skin with horny scales or horny plates.

Photo left: The Striped Basilisk is a very agile climber.

Photo above: This Bearded Dragon vividly calls to mind its saurian ancestors.

Photo above: All Crevice Spiny Lizards require a high temperature in their basking areas.

The Leopard Gecko clearly shows how it got its name.

Photo above: Bearded Dragons live in desert climates and like to rest on warm rocks.

Photo left: Two Tokay Geckos—they do not always get along so peaceably.

Photo above: A young Red-bellied Side-necked Turtle rests on the leaves of an aquatic plant.

Photo above: A strikingly colored Corn Snake, which can grow to be 71 inches (180 cm) long.

Photo above: This New Guinea Snake-necked Turtle is obviously enjoying its sunbath.

Photo left: The Garter Snake lives in areas of North America.

Striped Basilisk (continued)
Housing: Rain forest terrarium 32 × 24 × 39 inches (80 × 60 × 100 cm).
Decoration: Climbing branches, stumps, water basin, tough-leaved plants.
Temperature: Daytime 77 to 86°F (25–30°C), 68 to 77°F (20–25°C) at night, basking site, UV light.
Humidity: 60 to 90 percent.
Feeding: Three times a week: insects, chopped fish, earthworms, newborn mice, occasionally vegetarian food.
Similar to care for: **Knight Anole** Anolis equestris (see page 24), 22 inches (55 cm), head-body length 8 inches (20 cm), Cuba, Florida.
Special note: Adhesive lamellae, does not swim.
Tokay Gecko Gekko gecko (see page 56), 14 inches (35 cm), head-body length 7 inches (17 cm), southeastern Asia, nocturnal.

Garter Snake
Thamnophis sirtalis (see photo, page 21)
Total length: 39 inches (100 cm).
Habitat: North America, forest, scrubland, damp areas, always near water.
Behavior: Peaceful, diurnal, likes to swim, captures prey even in water, viviparous.
Housing: Aquaterrarium 49 × 30 × 20 inches (125 × 75 × 50 cm), about 2/3 land area, water depth 4 to 8 inches (10–20 cm).

Decoration: Climbing branches, stumps, emergent and submergent aquatic and climbing plants.
Temperature: Daytime 65 to 86°F (18–30°C), 65°F (18°C) at night, during rest period from November to February 59 to 65°F (15–18°C).
Humidity: 70 to 95 percent.
Feeding: Once a week: fish, earthworms, newborn mice.
Similar to care for: **Ribbon Snake** Thamnophis sauritus, 32 inches (80 cm), eastern North America.

Corn Snake
Elaphe guttata (see page 21)
Total length: 47 inches (120 cm).
Habitat: North America, forest, scrubland, cultivated areas.
Behavior: Peaceful, diurnal, likes to climb.
Housing: Forest terrarium 47 × 24 × 47 inches (120 × 60 × 120 cm).
Decoration: Climbing

The home of the Corn Snake is North America, where it lives in woodlands, scrublands, and cultivated areas.

branches, stumps, tough-leaved plants, water dish.

Temperature: Daytime 65 to 86°F (18–30°C), 65°F (18°C) at night, during the rest period from November to February 59 to 65°F (15–18°C).

Humidity: 60 to 90 percent.

Feeding: Once a week: mice.

Similar to care for: **Russian Ratsnake** *Elaphe schrenckii*, 47 inches (120 cm), eastern Asia.

Tarantulas:
Mexican Redknee Tarantula

Brachypelma smithi (see photo, page 57)

Body length: 3 inches (7 cm).

Habitat: Mexico, desert and semidesert; digs burrows under rocks and into hillsides.

Behavior: Peaceful, defends itself by hair flicking, frequently outside its shelter.

Housing: Desert terrarium 8 × 12 × 12 inches (20 × 30 × 30 cm).

Decoration: Potting soil or loam, keep moist outside shelter.

Temperature: 72 to 81°F (22–27°C).

Humidity: 70 to 100 percent.

Feeding: Once a week: house crickets and field crickets.

Similar to care for: **Mexican Fireleg Tarantula** *Brachypelma boehmei*.

TIP

Conservation Laws

Only species that may be kept, bred, and traded are presented in the descriptions in this guide. Terrarium animals sold in pet stores comply with the requirements of conservation laws and can be purchased legally. In order to be on the safe side, you should request a receipt showing the scientific name.

Please note that the legal regulations and the protection categories of individual species change from state to state, and those species designated as federally endangered may not be shipped interstate without permits. You can find out about the current status from the dealers, in specialized magazines, and from nature conservation authorities.

Specialty dealers are a reliable source for obtaining species. They often deal directly with breeders worldwide and import directly. Their specimens are usually acclimated, well fed, and checked by a veterinarian. Such dealers sell through mail order purchase and shipping, but many also buy and sell specimens at reptile and amphibian expos, which are held in a number of large cities in the United States.

CAGE FURNITURE AND TERRARIUM TECHNOLOGY

For many, the terrarium forms an integrated whole only if the animals and plants come from the same natural habitat. Provided that you observe a few basic rules, you can give your imagination free rein with cage furniture.

Cage Types

In principle, a terrarium can be set up anywhere, since with the appropriate technology (see page 28), the necessary conditions can be created in the living room just as well as in the basement or heated greenhouse. I advise against homemade terraria, and besides, a good pet store stocks ready-made terraria in styles and sizes to suit every purpose. Incidentally, terraria do not always have to be rectangular or horizontal; corner tanks, vertical tanks, or tanks with curved fronts are available.

Size

There are no generally mandatory standard dimensions for a terrarium, since the particular space required is determined by the size and behavior of the animals (see animal descriptions, beginning on page 14). Terraria most frequently available in pet stores have a width to depth to height ratio of approximately 2:1:1, for example, 32 × 16 × 16 inches (80 × 40 × 40 cm).

The Knight Anole uses adhesive lamellae to get a secure foothold in a rain forest terrarium.

Tarantula terraria should not have a surface area greater than 12 × 20 inches (30 × 50 cm); the height depends on the habits of the particular occupants.

Terrarium for climbing species: For animals that live in trees and climb on rocks, it is a good idea to make greater use of the height and change the ratio to 1:1:2.

Terrarium for terrestrial species: For purely ground-dwelling animals, a shallow terrarium with the proportions 2:2:1 is most suitable.

Terrarium for aquatic species: For water-dwelling species, an aquarium with the ratio 2:1:1 is recommended.

Glass or Plastic?

All-glass terraria held together with silicone sealant are preferable. However, the widely available plastic terraria with slotted lids are suitable for temporary housing in a pinch. Re-equipped with a screen cover so that light, heat, and UV radiation get into the container, they can be used as rearing and quarantine terraria (see Quarantine, page 12).

Air Circulation

Since nowhere is there so little movement of air as in a completely enclosed space, you must provide for sufficient air flow in the terrarium. For ventilation, there should be a perforated area of at least 10 percent in the lower third of either the front or the side as well as in the lid. As soon as heat sources warm the air in the terrarium, it begins to move, rises, and pulls in cooler air. For solid tanks, a small fan blowing across the screen top will do.

Which Type of Terrarium?

Because of the limited adaptability of terrarium animals (see Body Temperature, page 53), you have to pay very close attention to proper climate control and design of the environment. The more naturalistic living conditions you provide, the closer this comes to proper husbandry for the animal.
Note: There are fluid boundaries and many transitions between the following terrarium types.

The Rain Forest Terrarium

The most beautiful miniature landscapes can be created in a terrarium of this kind if it measures at least 32 × 16 × 16 inches (80 × 40 × 40 cm).

Plants: They can grow on the ground (terrestrial plants), but the more useful types grow on the walls and in branches (epiphytes) (see illustration, page 34). When choosing, take into consideration the weight and size of the animals (see animal descriptions, beginning on page 14), since plants can't

bear the weight of some animals.

Basking areas: For basking reptiles, plan plant-free basking spots that are warmed by standard spotlights (see page 29).

Plant wall: Usable space can be greatly increased by means of a plant wall, since the animals can also occupy the appropriately structured back and side walls (see HOW TO: Setting Up, pages 34–35).

The Desert Terrarium

The barren habitat typical of a desert terrarium is more difficult to present attractively. But with rocks, wood, sand, and arid-land plants, you can create charming landscape details.

Rocks: Look around outside. You can learn from nature how rock formations have grown. With skillful arrangement, additional hiding places and climbing areas can be created on the back and side walls.
Note: Under no circumstances interrupt the supply of fresh air!

Planting: You can also plant the dry terrarium, but only if you can provide the plants with water without at the same time soaking the entire bottom of the tank. Decorating with xerophytes such as grasses or broom (*Cutisus scoparis*) is more practical. Here you can let your imagination run free.

Animals from hot habitats need heated basking sites, but also many areas to which they can retreat.

The Aquaterrarium

Although—or precisely, because—water is the defining element here, this type of terrarium can be designed in a wide variety of ways.

Aquaterrarium for aquatic species: This is an aquarium with emergent and submergent aquatic plants (see Plant Selection, page 30). If the tank is filled only enough so that a space of 4 to 8 inches (10–20 cm) remains between tank edge and water level, you can place epiphytes here and put in climbing plants with aquatic roots (see Table, page 31) that will grow over the edge and, with a support, cover the background as well.

Aquaterrarium with dry areas: An aquaterrarium for animals that do not live exclusively in the water requires a distinctly lower water level. They need resting places outside the water in order to dry off occasionally under a spotlight. These could be islandlike structures in the water, a piece of bogwood jutting out of the water, or a shelf of perforated plastic secured over the water surface. If there is enough space remaining above the water, an epiphyte branch can be put in.

Aquaterrarium with damp island: In a tank with a water depth of 4 to 8 inches (10–20 cm), a slightly higher island can be created from flat slate or sandstone slabs, on which is placed a layer of moss in contact with the water. Climbing plants with aquatic roots can be placed so that they emerge from the water and grow over supports like osmunda fiber on the walls (see HOW TO: Setting Up, pages 34–35) and bogwood roots.

Aquaterrarium with land areas: Water depth of 4 to 8 inches (10 to 20 cm), but covering only about one third of the surface area. Plants in the water, creeping terrestrial plants and climbers on the land area, and epiphytes on the branches structure an aquarium of this sort.

Maintaining water quality: The greater the water volume, the more effort is required for water changes. Therefore, the installation of a filter is recommended for a water volume of 13 gallons (50 L) or more. However, there is no rule governing the interval between water changes, which are still necessary; you must acquire experience. Smaller water areas require more frequent changes.

Turtle resting on a root stump in a typical habitat.

Terrarium Technology

Since your pets come almost exclusively from tropical or subtropical zones, you must make sure the climate of your terrarium stays within the correct parameters. All the necessary equipment is sold in the pet store.

Note: With electrical devices, pay attention to the dangers that come particularly from working with electricity and water (see Important Note, page 63).

Heating

✔ Spotlights are good sources of heat and light for diurnal animals.

✔ For crepuscular and nocturnal animals as well as species from shady habitats, ceramic infrared heat lamps are suitable.

Note: If it is not possible to mount the lamps outside the terrarium, they must be equipped with a wire basket protector in order to safeguard the animals from burns.

Substrate heating: Supplemental heating may be necessary for one third of the cage bottom at most if:

✔ the location of the terrarium does not guarantee a minimum temperature at night after the heat lamp has been turned off;

✔ higher humidity should be achieved in an unplanted terrarium by means of evaporation;

✔ the substrate of a basking spot should receive extra heat. Substrate heaters are sold as hot rocks, heating cables, or heating pads with a low surface temperature. Heat pads that fit under the tank are safest. Cover heating cables or pads inside the tank with chromium steel screen (5 to 10 mm mesh) so that burrowing animals do not damage them.

Water heating: Submersible aquarium heaters (50 to 300 watts) can be mounted and protected from jostling by installing them in a perforated clay pipe or hollow rock. This is rarely necessary.

Temperature and Humidity

Variations between daytime and nighttime temperatures of 59°F (15°C) are not unusual in tropical regions. Humidity can also fluctuate considerably due to precipitation and temperature changes. Both must be monitored and controlled for proper climate control in the terrarium. Temperature drops of 41 to 50°F (5–10°C) at night as well as temperature reductions during the winter months can noticeably increase the vitality and life expectancy of the animals in the terrarium.

Timers: To control the day-night rhythm, use a commercially available timer that switches off the light and heat at night.

Thermometer: Simple room or digital thermometers can be used to monitor the temperature, but a minimum-maximum thermometer is best.

Bearded Dragons grow to 22 inches (55 cm) in length and are native to Australia.

Thermostat: From simple bimetallic instruments to electronic control systems with digital display, all sorts of devices are available for regulating temperature. Check to see that they are working by comparing temperatures every once in a while.

Hygrometer: Some models require no adjustment but are less accurate than the adjustable, more expensive models. If you buy an adjustable model, occasional activation of the hair strands is important for measuring atmospheric humidity. Constant monitoring is necessary at the very beginning.

Regulating humidity: Cage humidity can be increased by watering the plants and moistening the substrate, which can be heated slightly if necessary. Decrease cage humidity by using a small water dish, sand or gravel substrate instead of soil, and a screen top.

Lighting

Light is one of the basic requirements of life. Diurnal animals from tropical or subtropical regions will need plenty of light in the terrarium.

Fluorescent lamps are ideal for all terraria up to a height of 28 inches (70 cm). They are economical and efficient, and are available from the pet store in many sizes. Look for good color rendition.

Spotlights are good as heat-producing light sources, especially to create so-called hot spots for basking. As the sole source of light and heat, they are used only in very hot, dry desert terraria. The heat they produce makes them very susceptible to breaking from jarring or water splashes.

Mercury vapor and metal halide lamps are used by many hobbyists. Not only are they extremely bright, but they also give off a lot of heat and are therefore recommended only for larger sized cages.

UV lamps have a stimulating effect on many

A Tiger Salamander can keep its footing even on algae-covered rocks.

biological processes. UV-B light is important for the regulation of calcium metabolism, UV-A light for pigment formation in the skin. However, ultraviolet light seems to be of little or no importance for most nocturnal amphibians or for nocturnal and crepuscular reptiles.

Filtration

In an aquaterrarium with a water volume of 13 gallons (50 L) or more, it is advisable to filter the water. Power filters in various sizes and performance levels are available in the pet store. Filtration, however, does not eliminate the need for regular water changes (see HOW-TO: Care, pages 38–39).

Plants and Decoration

Living amid growing plants improves the well-being of terrarium animals—whether they are looking for opportunities to climb or seeking a safe place to hide.

Choosing the Right Plants

Only when you have determined that the animals under consideration are not vegetarians and are not too heavy can you begin to think about plants. Bright green species and those with tender or colorful leaves are more delicate than dark green plants with tough foliage. Comparatively few plants are suitable for our purposes, and these can be subdivided into terrestrial plants, ground covers, climbing plants, and epiphytes, as well as submergent (growing under the water) and emergent (growing above the water surface) aquatic plants.

Substrate Materials

The humidity level in the terrarium depends largely on the substrate. Sand absorbs comparatively little water; potting soil from broad-leaved and coniferous trees store a lot of water, which evaporates when warmed.

✔ River sand in various particle sizes is equally well suited for desert terraria and the water area of an aquaterrarium.

✔ Leaf litter not only offers the animals protection, but they can also occupy themselves naturally while searching for live prey.

✔ Amphibians in particular are happy on damp, but not wet, peat moss.

Decorative Rocks

✔ Granites are often interestingly colored, but very hard and therefore difficult to shape.

✔ Sandstones and slates can be shaped quite well and are available in many shapes and colors.

✔ Lava is very porous and therefore relatively simple and good to work, but also gets very dirty easily.

✔ Limestone increases water hardness and is not suitable for aquaterraria.

Attractive Woods

Locusts, lilacs, fruit trees, oaks, and vines offer branches for climbing and epiphytes that are interestingly shaped and at the same time sturdy. Root stumps on the cage bottom and bogwood in the water are decorative and provide shelter for the animals.

With the adhesive lamellae on its fingers and toes, a Tokay Gecko can find a foothold everywhere.

Easy-care Plants for the Terrarium

* = dry; ** = semidry; *** = moist; ~ = acquatic plant; +++ = a vary large amount of light' ++ = plenty of light; + = less light

Name	Habitat	Location	Light	Height	Remarks
Aglaonemas *Aglaonema* species	SE Asia	***	+	Up to 20 inches (50 cm)	Terrestrial, herbaceous, small species are especially suitable, easy to propagate
Aloes *Aloe* species	Africa	*	+++	Up to 24 inches (60 cm)	Terrestrial, succulent, small species are suitable
Sansevierias *Sansevieria* species	Africa	**	+++	Up to 24 inches (60 cm)	Terrestrial, low-growing species are highly suitable
Bromeliads *Aechmea* species	C + S Am	***, **	+++	16 inches (40 cm)	Epiphyte, [stiff,] only for larger terrariums
Bromeliads *Tillandsia* species	America	***, **	+++	2 to 12 inches (5 to 30 cm)	Epiphyte, grows very well without planting medium
Hornwort *Ceratophyllum demersum*	Tezw	~	+++	Up to 40 inches (100 cm)	Submergent, water level must be at least 4 inches (10 cm), has no roots, grows free in the water
Creeping Fig *Ficus pumila*	SE Asia	***	+	Leaves 3/4-inch (2 cm)	Climbing plant, grows better on damp stone, wood, or osmunda fiber than in soil
Benjamin Fig *Ficus benjamina*	SE Asia	***, **	+++	Up to 200 inches (500 cm)	Terrestrial, treelike; for larger terraria, choose small species
Gasterias *Gasteria* species	Africa	*	+++	Up to 8 inches (20 cm)	Terrestrial, succulent, uncomplicated
Haworthias *Haworthia* species	Africa	*	+++	4 inches (10 cm)	Terrestrial, succulent, uncomplicated
Golden Pothos *Epipremnum pinnatum*	SE Asia	***	+	Leaves up to 12 inches (30 cm)	Climbing plant, usually fairly small, aerial and aquatic roots, easy to propagate
Java Moss *Vesicularia dubyana*	SE Asia	~	+	Leaves 1/8 inch (3 mm)	Submergent, adheres to wood, rocks, and terrarium floor
Asparagus ferns *Asparagus* species	Africa	**	++	Up to 20 inches (50 cm)	Terrestrial, herbaceous, also grows hanging
Philodendrons *Philodendron* species	C + S Am	**	+	Leaves 2 to 20 inches (5 to 50 cm)	Climbing plant, aerial and aquatic roots, small species easy to propagate
Palm Fern *Blechnum gibbum*	SE Asia	***	++	12 inches (30 cm)	Terrestrial, herbaceous
Spathiphyllums *Spathiphyllum* species	S Am	***	++	8 to 20 inches (20 to 50 cm)	Terrestrial, herbaceous, blooms freely
Nephrolepis *Nephrolepis* species	SE Asia	***	++	Up to 16 inches (40 cm)	Terrestrial, herbaceous, avoid waterlogging and bottom heat
Epiphytic cacti *Rhipsalis and Lepismium* species	C + S Am	***	+++	12 inches (30 cm)	Epiphyte, grows hanging; not suitable for larger, heavy reptiles

S Am = South America; C Am = Central America; SE Asia = Southeast Asia; Tezw = temperate zones worldwide

PORTRAITS:
TERRARIUM PLANTS

For every habitat there are a variety of typical plants you can use to create a natural environment for your terrarium animals and at the same time put decorative accents in the terrarium.

Photo above: Spiderwort (Tradescantia), *South America.*

Photo left: Spurge (Euphorbia), *Africa.*

Photos above (from left to right):
Benjamin Fig (Ficus), *southeast Asia.*
Calathea (Calathea), *Central and South America.*
Maranta (Maranta), *Central and South America.*

Aglaonema (Aglaonema), *southeast Asia.*

Photo left: Water Lettuce (Pistia stratiotes), *tropical zones worldwide.*

Photo above: Echereria (Echeveria), *Central America.*

Photo right: Neoregelia (Neoregelia), Central and ~~uth~~ *America.*

Photo above: Prickly Pear (Opuntia), *Central America.*

Photo left: Blooming mammillaria cactus (Mammillaria), Central and South America.

Echereria (Echeveria), *Central America.*

In designing a terrarium, there are almost no limits placed on your imagination if you observe a few basic rules:

✔ While making things as naturalistic as possible, you cannot lose track of certain basics. For instance, it must be possible to remove droppings and uneaten food without difficulty.
✔ Install rockwork—backgrounds, caves, basking spots—firmly and immovably on the tank bottom using silicone aquarium sealant. If the rocks shift, they can shatter the glass walls and injure your pets.
✔ Crossing branches, improperly aligned sections, splintered trunks, and open loops of wire can lead to injuries.
✔ Install all technical equipment out of sight but still easily accessible. Above all, monitors and controllers should be easy to read.
✔ Under no circumstances should you block ventilation gratings.

Curved pieces of bark make especially good hiding places.

Creating Hiding Places

Animals find good places to hide in hollow sections of tree trunk or curved sections of cork bark. If the log is cut flat on one side and placed with the cut surface against the front glass, you can easily observe what is going on inside. If the animals show signs of fear at the exposure, or reluctance to use the hiding area, move the cave far away enough from the glass so that timid animals always have a place to hide.

Constructing a Plant Wall

Fasten hardware cloth or large mesh plastic netting, 1/4- to 1/2-inch (6–13 mm) mesh, on a frame that you glue to the side or back wall with silicone sealant. Stuff soil/moss or soil/peat moss mixture evenly behind the mesh.

Put in the plants: Insert cuttings of climbing plants directly into the wall. Use wire or plastic plant clips to attach shoots without roots or that have not yet rooted. Arrange them so that the lower area receives sufficient light.

Substrate for climbing plants: Slabs of osmunda fiber have outstanding properties as a substrate for climbing plants. This material, made of tree fern, is glued while dry to the walls of the container using silicone sealant. Kept evenly moist, it is the ideal support.

Provide epiphyte branches with drainage holes so that there is no waterlogging.

There must be a clear separation between water and land areas.

Setting Up a Pool
✔ Place the bathing pool basin on the drainage layer, since an occasional spill cannot be ruled out.
✔ In the aquaterrarium with land area, make a clear separation between the water and land by placing a glass panel of the appropriate height between the two areas and gluing it in place with silicone sealant.
✔ Do not set drinking water dishes on the substrate, but rather, embed them in it.

Planting Epiphytes
Epiphytes or "air plants" can be planted in forks or cavities of branches or on pieces of wood:
✔ For this purpose, it is best to choose hard, moisture-resistant branches of fruit trees, lilacs, or locusts.
✔ You can drill planting holes in larger branches. Fasten the epiphytes to smaller branches with wire or fishing line. Simply press them into cavities.
✔ Free the root ball from the surrounding loose soil, pack it in moss or some other water-permeable planting medium, moisten well, and either tie on or press in.
✔ Keep evenly moist. The water must be able to run off easily, since epiphytes do not tolerate waterlogging.

Substrate Planting
✔ Put in a layer of gravel 1 to 2 inches (3–5 cm) deep for drainage, particle size 5 to 10 mm.

✔ Cover the gravel with wire or plastic screen so that burrowing animals cannot root up everything.
✔ Depending on the size of the plants, add potting soil from broad-leaved or coniferous trees to a depth of 1-1/2 to 6 inches (3 to 15 cm).
✔ Put the root balls in planting holes.

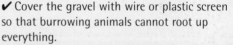

When constructing the plant wall, never block the ventilation holes.

ROUTINE TERRARIUM MAINTENANCE

Proper husbandry of terrarium animals requires not only a great deal of intuition, but first and foremost, a readiness to gain experience. Observing attentively and using those observations is the basis of terrarium maintenance.

Skin Care

Terrarium animals do not require grooming as do dogs and horses. Instead, you must pay attention to shedding of the skin, or molting (ecdysis), and see that it progresses normally (see pages 54–55).

Note: In order to become acquainted with the shedding behavior of your pets, you should note down all observations carefully.

If complications arise in reptiles—perhaps because the air in the terrarium is too dry, there are developmental or metabolic disorders, or a stress situation has arisen because of a change of location—you must provide immediate support.

Help with Shedding

In snakes: If shedding is incomplete or if the skin comes off in patches, soak the snake for several hours in a shallow, tepid, water-filled bucket or a plastic container—in each case with a perforated lid. If it still does not shed its skin in water, let the reptile crawl through your

The photo clearly shows why this amphibian is called the Fire-bellied Toad.

tightly closed hand, with which you can apply gentle pressure and in this way help the animal get rid of its skin.

With lizards: Here you can help by misting frequently with water, at least three times a day, and removing the softened shreds of skin with tweezers. But proceed carefully and spray into the air *above* the lizard, not onto the lizard.

Care of the Claws

If climbing lizards do not have adhesive lamellae on the undersides of finger and toes, they need long sharp claws in order to keep their footing everywhere. If the claws of terrestrial lizards and turtles are too long and curved, however, they must be trimmed. In addition to sand or leaves, try putting a stone slab into the terrarium, since insufficient wear along with inadequate activity is responsible for excessively long claws.

Trimming claws: You can trim the claws with a pair of heavy-duty nail clippers (see illustration, page 38). Beginners should definitely have a veterinarian, pet dealer, or experienced herpetoculturist demonstrate this technique.

Cleaning Utensils

For regular cleaning jobs, tweezers (1,2), shovel (3), brush (or sponge) (4), putty knife (5), and paper towels are required. Always clean thoroughly after use. If you use the same utensils for several terraria, disinfect them very carefully each time before moving on to the next tank, since the danger of infections and parasites varies in individual species.

Daily Maintenance Tasks

✔ Remove feces and urine.
✔ Fill water dish with fresh water.
✔ Smooth churned-up substrate.
✔ Remove uneaten food. In order to prevent the spread of infections, never feed leftovers to other animals in other terraria.
✔ Mist plants and remove dead leaves. Always mist at the beginning of the activity period; plants and animals will be refreshed by the "dew" (see illustration, page 47).
✔ Clean terrarium glass.
✔ Feed as needed.

Watering the Plants

To water the plants, use only clean rainwater or desalinated water, which you can buy or prepare yourself using ion exchange or reverse osmosis units (pet store). In order to prevent compaction and flooding of the substrate, water the plants using commercially available spray bottles (or atomizers) (7). Adjust the temperature of the water to that in the terrarium. Do not add fertilizer.

Plant Pests

Chemical pesticides should not be used in the terrarium. The best action to take is replacement of the infested plants.

Cutting Claws

Trim excessively long claws only in terrestrial lizards; climbing lizards need long sharp claws in order to find a foothold everywhere.

When trimming claws, do not cut into the blood vessels!

Changing the Terrarium Substrate

At the very latest, it is time to change the substrate when the initially fresh earthy smell changes. The substrate can sour depending on the number of animals in the tank, and it can also become soggy due to excessive watering of plants or overflowing of the water dish. In such cases, remove it completely and replace it with new substrate.

Temporary relocation of the animals: While changing the substrate or putting in new decorations and plants, the animals are temporarily relocated (see Catching Terrarium Animals, page 40). An escape-proof box can serve as a temporary home for a few hours.

Changing the Water

As soon as the water in an aquaterrarium is fouled by feces or uneaten food, it must be changed. Use a siphon to remove the fouled water, or use a small container to bail out the water. Once the dirty water has been completely removed, add fresh water. Use a thermometer so you can add warm or cold water for the correct temperature.
Note: For reasons of hygiene, never use your mouth to start the siphon in the hose.

Forced Restraint

For turtles: In order to give a turtle (vitamin) drops, hold the animal on its back and put the droplet on the tip of its chin; the droplet will trickle from there between the horny jaws into the mouth.

For snakes and lizards: To treat diseases, for instance to give medication, put the animal in a cloth bag (6) so that only the head

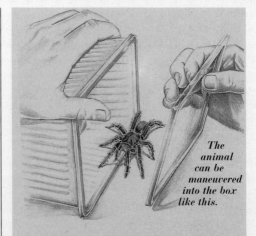

The animal can be maneuvered into the box like this.

When Tarantulas Must Be Temporarily Relocated

Even a beginner can catch a tarantula quite simply and safely in this manner using a plastic box.

sticks out and restrain bag and neck with one hand while the rest of the reptile's wriggling body is confined in the bag.
Note: Caution notwithstanding, sharp claws can scratch dangerously even through the cloth. See a physician in case of injury (see page 63).

This is how a turtle can be given drops easily.

African Five-lined Skinks come from central Africa and like suitably dry habitats.

Catching Terrarium Animals

From time to time you will be forced to catch one of your animals and hold on to it correctly. That is not always easy, because they may be slippery, fast, and able to put up a fight.

Aquatic amphibians: Catch them with a net and cup your hand over the top. If they must be held tightly (restrained), this is also done most safely in the net because it is easier to get a good grip on them through the material.

Terrestrial amphibians: Either catch and restrain them with the net as well, grasp them from above around their waist, or shoo them like a tarantula into a box or a glass.

Tarantulas: Any tarantula can be herded simply and quite safely into a commercially available critter cage (see drawing, page 39).

Turtles: Hold them by the shell. Be careful with biting individuals. Grasp these by the shell in the area of the back legs so that even long-necked species cannot reach your fingers.

Smaller lizards: For small to medium-size lizards, grasp the neck swiftly and surely from above with the thumb and index finger of one hand and restrain the head with a firm grip on each side. With the free fingers, clasp the body of the animal.

Note: Be careful with species that can lose the tail, like geckos (see page 53). Here the hand encircles the tail very gently.

Large lizards: While one hand clasps the neck, the other holds the pelvis and immobilizes the extended rear legs. With a large lizard that is putting up a fight, also secure the front legs with the hand holding the neck, because kicking, sharp-clawed feet can cause nasty lacerations.

Snakes: Snakes can be grasped and held like lizards, but in this case you have to deal with a long, powerfully writhing body. In contrast to the lizards, which generally take flight, snakes unaccustomed to handling assume a defensive posture and may bite.

Note: Cover the snake with a cloth in order to disorient it and grab through the cloth.

10 Golden Rules
for Care

1 Proper care and hygiene are not only good for the health of the animals, you protect yourself in this way as well.

2 Do not do any more work in the terrarium than necessary, because it may have a disturbing effect.

3 As the animals become acclimated, their nervousness decreases, but still, every disturbance means stress.

4 During the acclimation period, clean the terrarium glass only when the dirt really becomes annoying.

5 If the area around the terrarium is visible at a glance, this makes care easier and helps to prevent breakdowns and accidents.

6 Always close doors and lids of terraria carefully so that no one can reach in unsupervised, but also so that none of the animals can escape.

7 Escaped terrarium animals can cause fear and panic and have little chance of surviving outside the terrarium.

8 Remove feces and urine, and check the consistency of the feces in the process. If feces get in the water bowl, change the water completely; otherwise, add fresh water.

9 In general, mist plants rather than water them. Clean rainwater or desalinated water from the pet store is best, but most tap water would serve this purpose.

10 In the unplanted rain forest terrarium, provide for humidity by spraying water.

CARE DURING VACATION

When you go on vacation during the winter months, you can ease the work of your caretaker if you lower the temperature in your temperate terrarium to about 41°F (5°C). This places the temperate-area species in a pseudo-rest.

✔ *Turn off all heaters and lamps; only the light necessary for plants remains unchanged. In this way, food intake—and with it, fouling— ceases entirely or to a large extent.*

✔ *Make sure that the terrarium does not heat up due to sunlight falling on it. If so, the animals and plants will need considerably more water.*

✔ *Clean the terraria thoroughly the day before departure; do not feed the animals any more after that.*

✔ *Feed aquatic turtles and amphibians reduced amounts two weeks before the trip so that there will be less excrement and it will not be necessary to change the water.*

✔ *Spare your substitute the task of administering vitamins and minerals.*

✔ *It is important to note that tropical species may be severely stressed by protracted lowered light and temperature levels.*

Feeding

Some of the animals presented in our guide—the so-called omnivores—eat both animal and plant food. In the Portraits (see beginning on page 14) you will find detailed recommendations for the preferred diet of specific animals.

Watering animals: Pets in the aquaterrarium are provided with drinking water. In the rain forest terrarium, the "dew" (see page 47) is used as drinking water. For all other animals, the water dish, which is part of the cage furniture, is both bathtub and drinking bowl. A standard water dish belongs in every tarantula terrarium.

Plant Food

Fruits and vegetables: Food from your own garden or from an organic grower is always highly nutritious. Generally speaking, fruit grown and naturally ripened in our latitudes is preferable to exotic treats, because imported fruits are always harvested before they are ripe.

Grasses and weeds: The most nutritious food for herbivores and omnivores consists of wild grasses and weeds. Especially suitable are dandelions, plantain, clover, orache, and chickweed, including the flowers, of course. **Note:** Do not collect food plants from along heavily traveled roads, dumps, or other areas known to be contaminated with harmful substances (see meadow plankton, page 43).

Animal Food

A large portion of our pets are hunters and they should also have the opportunity to stalk live prey. We cannot feed predators, as these hunters are called, with only ground meat. Besides, meat alone is not good for any carnivore. Bones, hair, scales, chitin, and stomach contents of prey animals are of great importance for nutrition as well as for digestive processes. The selection of suitable live insects offered by the pet store ensures that you can always buy the required items in various sizes at any time.

Note: You can place a standing order for live foods with many dealers and have them delivered as arranged.

Small Mammals

Mice are required for snakes, but many lizards and large anurans opportunistically feed on mice of various sizes.

Aquatic Animals

✔ Freshwater fish such as goldfish, guppies, smelt, and trout, are not only easily digested, high-protein fare, but serve as an important source of readily accessible vitamins and minerals. Since it is not always possible to obtain fresh fish, you should have a supply stored in the freezer. A wholly frozen-fish diet can cause thiminase imbalance, so use fresh fish when available.

✔ Daphnia, mosquito larvae, and freshwater shrimp are excellent foods for small turtles, aquatic amphibians, and their larvae.

Note: Get permission from the landowner before going out with a net to catch your own food.

Insects and Arachnids

✔ House crickets and field crickets are eagerly accepted by many carnivores. They are also the ideal food for all tarantulas.

✔ Grasshoppers are an excellent food for larger pets.

✔ Fruit flies and their larvae are good for feeding to young lizards and tarantulas as well as small amphibians. During the summer months, these flies can be attracted with fruit.

✔ Aphids are the simplest natural food to obtain and an excellent choice for feeding small amphibians and reptiles.

✔ Meadow plankton is the general term for insects and arachnids that you can collect yourself by sweeping weedy meadows and edges of fields with an insect net.

Bearded Dragons as so-called omnivores also eat plants.

This young Knight Anole can grow to a head-body length of 8 inches (20 cm).

Incidentally, food plants that are largely unpolluted also grow in such habitats. The insects found there make up the most natural diet that insectivorous pets can be offered. But they must not be collected in protected areas, and there cannot be any protected plant species among the catch.
Note: Obtain information on land ownership and conservation regulations from the county or state government.

Worms

Earthworms are an important source of minerals because of the earthy contents of their stomachs. You can either collect the worms, dig them up in your own garden, or buy them at a bait shop.

Vitamins and Minerals

Vitamins are triggers for vital metabolic processes; they are ingested naturally with the food or produced during certain digestive processes.

Minerals such as calcium, phosphorus, and magnesium are used primarily for building bones and teeth. They are especially important to growing young animals.

Trace elements such as potassium, iron, iodine, fluorine, and selenium are important for the formation of enzymes and hormones.

Since terrariums provide a false environment, correct vitamin and mineral levels generally need to be augmented.

If there are clear signs of deficiency such as swollen eyelids and rickets (see page 50), direct administration of supplements can also be indicated.

Vitamin and mineral supplements for terrarium animals are available as drops and as powder in the pet store and as multivitamin preparations in the pharmacy or from the veterinarian, who will also tell you the dosage. Drops are dripped directly into the animal's mouth; powder is mixed in with the food. Follow the directions.

Note: One method that has proven to be both simple and successful is to crumble eggshell or bird's cuttlebone and scatter some of it in the terrarium once a week. Many lizards and turtles eagerly devour the crumbs.

Force-feeding

If a reptile or amphibian refuses to eat for an unusually long time, by all means consult an experienced herpetoculturist before you resort to force-feeding. There is really no reliable opinion on tolerable fasting periods, since the times reported are immensely far apart, actually in the area of two weeks to two years.

For lizards and snakes, opening the mouth and putting in the food is not difficult (see HOW-TO: Feeding, page 47).

For turtles and amphibians, on the other hand, force-feeding requires so much skill and is associated with so much stress for the animals that under no circumstances should it be undertaken by novice terrarium keepers.

Checklist
Feeding

1 Water or mist in the morning; feed at the beginning of the activity period.

2 Provide a varied diet; foods with different colors and odors stimulate the appetite.

3 Naturally ripened, organically grown fruits and vegetables are better than those harvested before they are ripe.

4 Vitamins, minerals, and trace elements are important for metabolism, bones, and formation of enzymes and hormones.

5 Remove uneaten food in the evening, or for nocturnal pets, in the morning. Next time, offer less.

6 Do not feed uneaten food to animals in other terraria.

7 If force-feeding for the first time, seek advice beforehand.

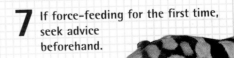

When and How Much to Feed

Generally speaking, food should be offered when the animals are active. Ask for advice when you buy an animal and learn through observation just how much your pets eat. The correct amount of food is what is eagerly devoured when feeding. Anything more is too much, because the animals should not be able to eat continuously, nor should there be any food left over. Some species have their own fasting periods; snakes and tarantulas, for example, do not eat during shedding.

How to Feed

Leaves and grasses are placed on the bottom of the terrarium, but avoid the area the animals

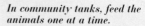
In community tanks, feed the animals one at a time.

prefer to use for defecating and urinating.

Prekilled food is introduced only after both the species and the size of the preferred prey have been determined beyond a doubt with the help of information from the dealer. Prekilled mice or rats are preferred because feeding live foods can be hazardous; terrarium animals have been bitten or killed by live prey animals.

If several animals are kept in one tank, it is safer, especially with snakes, to hold the prekilled prey in front of them with forceps in order to prevent disturbances caused by competition for food.

Feeder fish of the right size to be swallowed are put into the water, where predators will seize and devour them. Do not feed chopped fish as filets, but rather with scales, bones, and viscera. Thaw frozen food slowly and offer

In an aquaterrarium, the food is put directly into the water.

it only after it has warmed up.

Insects can be dusted easily with a vitamin-mineral mixture: Put a small amount of the mixture in a container or plastic bag, add the insects, close, and shake until the insects look like they are covered with flour. Then toss them to your pets one at a time so that they can be captured after a short chase, or else hold them in front of the animals with forceps so that they do not escape. **Note:** Remove uneaten insects, since they lose their nutrition value quickly.

Meadow plankton is placed directly in the terrarium. Because of the different climate, these invertebrates will not become established there.

Aphids are put in with the leaves and stems.

Earthworms are always offered under close supervision, or they crawl away and are lost as food.

Feeding in the aquaterrarium: Here the animals receive live and dead

When force-feeding, restrain the animal gently.

food in the water. Be especially precise when feeding, because any excess fouls the water in which they live.

Watering the Animals

Aquaterrarium: Here the animals are provided with drinking water—one more reason to change the water regularly.

Rain forest terrarium: Mist daily; the "dew" will be used by the animals as drinking water. Change drinking or bathing water three times a week.

Desert terrarium: The same applies for the desert terrarium, but mist only partially and less intensively. Change water in the small drinking bowl daily.

Tarantula terrarium: Replace water in drinking bowl every two to three days.

Many animals use the dew as drinking water.

Force-feeding

If a lizard or snake must be force-fed (see page 45), grasp the animal with the thumb and index finger of the left hand behind the head on either side. Hold the body of a prekilled small lizard or small mouse with the free fingers of the left hand.

Enclose the bodies of larger lizards and snakes in a cloth bag. If the animal opens its mouth in fright or defense, a wooden spatula, or better yet, a vaginal speculum (veterinary instrument), can be inserted into the mouth. If it doesn't do that, the free right hand—or a second person—must pry open the mouth gently, slip in the spatula or speculum, and then carefully introduce the food.

Diseases

The table on page 51 will provide you with information on signs of disease and their possible causes. Do not experiment yourself because time can be lost unnecessarily due to nonspecific or even incorrect treatments. Under no circumstances should you constantly administer small quantities of "preventive" medicines.

Preventive Measures

Quarantine: This is very important because terrarium animals are exposed to many stresses and possible infections on the way from their native habitat or their place of birth to you. Besides, you have the best opportunity to observe new animals in the quarantine terrarium (see page 12). This means not just looking for pathological changes, but also noting changes in behavior. Because the normal reactions of a new animal are not yet familiar to you, you should seek the advice of an experienced terrarium keeper.

Make notes on behavior: Daily records of all behaviors, including eating and digestion, are helpful. Important conclusions can also be drawn from temperature and humidity measurements.

Trade experiences: Find a veterinarian who will treat amphibian and reptilian diseases. He or she will also need to analyze fecal samples, something that should continue to be done annually. Since very few veterinarians specialize in tarantulas, when in doubt you should seek the advice of experienced tarantula keepers.

Digestive Tract Diseases

Visible changes in feces: Normally, the feces are pellet-shaped, brownish, or, if the diet includes grass and leaves, greenish in color, and do not have a noticeable odor. Depending on the food eaten, they contain hair, teeth, claws, chitin, plant fibers, and not infrequently, sand and small stones as well. If the feces are watery and slimy and have a penetrating odor, or if they contain blood, this indicates an intestinal injury.

Treatment: Collect fresh fecal samples and bring or send them immediately to your veterinarian. The veterinarian will initiate an appropriate treatment based on the results of the analysis.

Endoparasites: Apart from worms, which might be observed in freshly deposited feces when there is a heavy infestation, there are few symptoms of possible intestinal parasites. Fecal analyzation is important because endoparasites can cause emaciation, perforation, and inflammation of the digestive tract.

Corn Snakes are diurnal reptiles that—as seen here—like to climb on tree branches.

The Tokay Gecko comes from Asia and in the evening hours calls loudly "to-kay, to-kay."

Treatment: The veterinarian may detect amoebae, flagellates, tapeworms, roundworms, threadworms, or hairworms. He or she will prescribe the appropriate medications.

External Parasites

Mites: These blackish parasites that are the size of a pinhead live between the reptile's scales. Debilitation and stress due to itching and blood loss are the consequences. Mites on tarantulas are smaller and beige-colored.

Treatment:

✔ If you discover the infestation at the time of purchase, dip the transport bag in a 0.2 percent solution of trichlorfon or Ivermectin and leave the animal in the drying bag for a few hours.

✔ If you discover an infestation of mites in your terrarium, spray the animals as well as the container thoroughly with the solution.

✔ Treat infested reptiles with skin lesions and geckos by hanging one-inch (2.5 cm) squares of "no-pest" strips from the pet store near the top of the cage. Remove the water bowl during the three-day treatment.

✔ Treat tarantulas by repeated CO_2 showers in a closed container, clean the terrarium thoroughly, and replace the decorations.

Ticks: These arthropods, up to 3 mm long and extremely flattened, attach themselves firmly with their mouthparts under the scales and in the soft skin of the reptiles, and suck their blood.

Treatment: As for mite infestation. If use of trichlorfon or Ivermectin is not possible because of severe damage to the skin, dab the ticks with cod-liver oil ointment (in the quarantine terrarium). On a long-term basis, this can be successful.

Skin Diseases

Abscesses: The veterinarian lances the abscess, cleans out the wound, and prescribes treatment.

Fungal skin infection in reptiles: The veterinarian takes tissue samples and tries to find an effective medication. Treatment prolonged.

Fungal skin infection in amphibians: The disease usually occurs as the result of another frequently unrecognized skin disease in aquatic amphibians. Treat with preparations used for fungal infections in ornamental fish, following the directions.

Fungal skin infection in tarantulas: White furry coating. Try treatment with an antifungal ointment. Check the caging environment; it might be too humid.

External Injuries

Treat small wounds with antibiotic or sulfonamide powder or ointment. Do not apply bandages or dressings. House in the quarantine terrarium, kept as sterile as possible. For larger injuries, take the animal to the veterinarian. In tarantulas, to stop the bleeding from small tears in the abdomen due to crushing or falls, use liquid bandage.

Mouth Rot (Infectious Necrotic Stomatitis)

Swab with tincture of chamomile tea. Take the animal to the veterinarian. Give a multi-vitamin preparation to increase resistance.

Respiratory Infections

Infections are favored by inadequate climate control and stress. Activity and food intake are greatly reduced. Respiratory infections are treated by the veterinarian with antibiotics or sulfonamide. Resistance can be increased by administration of vitamins.

Eye Inflammations

The veterinarian will prescribe eyedrops for an inflammation and inject vitamins for swellings. As a supportive measure, give a multivitamin preparation daily for at least four weeks, following the directions.

Rickets

Along with various other causes (see page 51), an incorrect diet and insufficient space can cause metabolic problems, such as softening of the bones. Give high doses of multivitamins and calcium.

This is the correct way to pack lizards and other reptiles for transport.

Recognizing Diseases

Signs of Disease	Cause
Vomiting	Poor husbandry, quantity/size of food too large, poisoning
Feces watery, slimy, bloody, penetrating odor, cloaca inflamed, dirty	Inflammation of the digestive tract caused by bacterial or viral infection, parasites
Worms in feces	Intestinal parasites
Whitish gray encrustations on the skin	Mite infestation
Lens-shaped objects hanging on the skin	Tick infestation
Skin abscesses	Injuries, metabolic disturbances
Scabby skin lesions	Fungal skin infection, favored by excessively damp environmental conditions
White growths	Fungal skin infection
Deposits of cheesy material, abscesses, necrosis in mouth	Mouth rot (infectious necrotic stomatitis)
Bubbles around the nostrils, sudden opening of the mouth, wheezing	Respiratory infection
Tears, discoloration of the eyes	Inflammation caused by drafts, incorrect vitamin levels, burns caused by UV light
Swollen eyelids	Vitamin and mineral deficiency, unhygienic housing conditions
Skeletal deformities, soft shell	Rickets, metabolic disorders, poor husbandry
Injuries to the appendages and the abdomen in tarantulas	Fall from a height, improper handling

BEHAVIOR AND OBSERVATION

Over the course of their million-year history, our terrarium animals have adapted to their specific habitats and developed corresponding behavioral characteristics that make observing them in the terrarium an exciting experience.

Characteristics

Body Temperature

Amphibians, reptiles, and arachnids are ectothermic or cold-blooded animals in which the temperature of the blood is influenced by the temperature of the environment. Since their entire life cycle is controlled from the outside, we must observe, monitor, and regulate conditions for them much more closely than for warm-blooded animals.

The Skeleton

Skeleton: Amphibians and reptiles both have a skeleton. Amphibians' skeletons contain comparatively less calcium than those of reptiles, and therefore their bones are usually more elastic. In turtles, the backbone, ribs, parts of the shoulder girdle, and bony plates in the skin fused to form the rigid shell. The only moveable elements are the neck and tail vertebrae, and of course the legs.

Red-bellied Side-necked Turtles are social species living on stream banks in New Guinea.

Appendages:
✔ Arboreal lizards can be recognized by their extremely long limbs and sharp claws.
✔ Terrestrial species, in contrast, have short, muscular legs, frequently with powerful feet that are well suited for digging.
✔ Reptiles living in or near the water usually have webbing between the toes.
✔ Special features include the sticky pads on fingers and toes of tree frogs and the adhesive lamellae of many geckos.

Tail: Another anatomical adaptation to their living conditions is the ability of many lizards, in response to danger, to shed part or all of their tail. This act, called *autotomy*, serves as a defensive measure because the attacker is easily distracted by the discarded tail, especially since the tail fragment continues to wriggle for a while. Although a new tail grows again in place of the one thus cast off, it has only cartilaginous vertebrae.

Sensory Organs

Eyes: The ability to see differs among the individual species, depending on their lifestyle.
✔ Terrestrial anurans, for example, see well as predators, while aquatic species rely more on their sense of smell.

✔ Turtles and tortoises can distinguish colors very well and use this to recognize preferred flowers and fruits even from far away.

✔ Snakes and many lizards are more able to detect motion and depend on smell for anything else.

✔ Nocturnal and crepuscular terrarium animals have vertical pupils. This affords daytime protection to their eyes, which are adapted to dim light; with decreasing light intensity, the pupils dilate.

✔ In all snakes, most geckos, as well as some skinks and lizards, the eyelids have fused to form transparent "spectacles" or eyecaps. As part of the skin, the eyecaps must also be shed.

Tongue:

✔ Terrestrial anurans use their tongue for catching prey. It becomes sticky as it rubs along the intermaxillary glands on the roof of the mouth when it shoots forward.

✔ Most lizards and all snakes use their tongues to scent prey. Flicking in and out, the tongue absorbs scent molecules and transports them to the olfactory cells of the Jacobson's organ in the roof of the mouth.

✔ The tongue of snakes and many lizards is long and deeply forked, while in turtles and most amphibians, it is more or less short and thick.

✔ Many lizards use the tongue to clean the mouth thoroughly after eating; almost all reptiles use it to lap up water; geckos also lick their eyes.

The Skin

Tarantulas have two body parts: the anterior prosoma (cephalothorax), and the posterior opisthosoma (abdomen), which are protected by chitin plates.

Amphibians have soft, moist, glandular skin. The secretion of the glands prevents the skin from drying out, especially where the animals inhabit relatively dry habitats. If they are indigenous to damp environments, the glandular secretion also has a bactericidal and fungicidal effect and thus takes the place of the protection provided by a horny skin.

Reptiles, on the other hand, have leathery skin without cutaneous glands. The skin is dry to the touch. Consisting of scales of various sizes, sometimes heavily cornified, this type of body covering permits reptiles to live in drier areas than amphibians.

Shedding (Ecdysis)

Arachnids, amphibians, and reptiles shed their skin or molt regularly. Rapidly growing young animals outgrow their external covering more quickly, so they shed their skin more frequently than older ones. Shedding depends on season, climate, food supply, and general condition. It is controlled by hormones and is a striking process, whose approach is heralded by certain changes.

Tarantulas: To molt, the tarantula disappears into its hiding place, spins a web, and stops eating. After a few days, it lies on its back, and several hours later, slips out of its skin.

Amphibians: Although all amphibians shed their skin, the process, because it is more infrequent and less conspicuous, is often not even noticed.

✔ Anurans eat their skin as it is shed, the perfect reutilization of valuable building materials.

✔ Caudates lose their skin in inconspicuous patches.

Reptiles: Shedding is a striking process that in snakes is preceded by a noticeable cloudiness of the eyes. A week or so later, the skin is usually shed in one piece. In lizards, the skin comes off in patches (see illustration, page 54), and in many species shedding takes weeks. Some turtle species also shed the outer layer of each horny scute.

The Tarantula's Venomous Bite

Some American species of tarantulas defend themselves by "hair flicking." To do this, the spider brushes fine hairs from its abdomen toward its attacker with quick movements of the hind legs (see Interpreting Behavior, page 57); these urticating hairs not only cause an unpleasant irritation of the skin and mucous membranes, but can also get into the

respiratory tract. Most tarantulas, however, defend themselves with their venomous bite. On their cephalothorax there are four walking legs on either side, two pedipalps in the front, and between these the chelicerae. These consist of the proximal segment with the venom glands and the fangs, through which the venom is injected into the prey. For humans, the bite is painful, but not life-threatening. The risk of blood poisoning due to bacteria transmitted by the chelicerae cannot, however, be ruled out. And in allergic individuals, a potentially fatal shock can be triggered by the venomous bite (see Important Note, page 63). These people are also particularly sensitive to the urticating hairs broadcast by hair flicking.

The Leopard Gecko eats its old skin—a perfect recycling of valuable materials.

For the proper care of a terrarium animal, you must be able to interpret its appearance as well as its behavior.

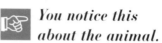 You notice this about the animal.

❓ What does it mean for the keeper?

❗ This is how to respond correctly to it.

🖐 Adhesive lamellae provide a foothold.

❓ Put in large-leaved plants.

❗ If the animal cannot find a foothold, assistance with shedding is necessary.

The body color of the Giant Toad is marbled brown.

❓ Clue to the color and structure of the habitat.

❗ Use leaf mold as a substrate in the terrarium.

🖐 Some Geckos attach their eggs to a communal laying site.

❓ The incubation conditions are favorable here.

❗ Leave the eggs there and cover them.

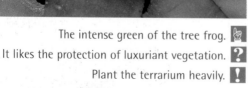

The intense green of the tree frog. 🖐
It likes the protection of luxuriant vegetation. ❓
Plant the terrarium heavily. ❗

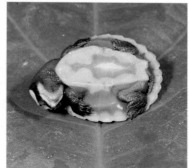

🖐 A Red-bellie Side-neck Turtle lays its head along its body.

❓ The animal a so-called side-necked turtle.

❗ This is a display of norm behavior.

Bearded Dragons live in groups with social behavior.

Communication among members of the species is necessary.

Watch out for incompatibility; keep only one male in a cage.

Sticky pads on fingers and toes of tree frogs.

They are indicative of a life on leaves.

Decorate with large-leaved, sturdy plants.

Tarantula kicks hairs from its abdomen.

The spider feels threatened.

Fewer disturbances, more cover.

Crevice Spiny Lizards live in small groups.

Sociality is vital.

Terrarium with at least four animals, but only one male.

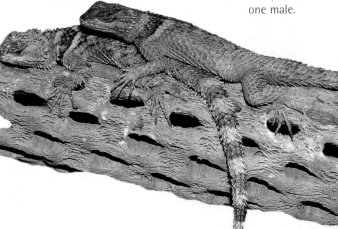

Bearded Dragon threatens with inflated beard.

Breeding display; disturbance by keeper.

Remove the disturbance, watch for aggressive behavior.

Reproduction and Breeding

In order to trigger the reproductive cycle, optimal husbandry is required. Often, day length, climate, or climatic changes are crucial triggers. Since clear-cut sex determination is often difficult, as a beginner you should ask the advice of an experienced terrarium keeper. In many cases, the differences are noticeable only during the breeding period.

Tarantulas: Usually housed separately, they can be brought together for mating. However, breeding tarantulas requires a great deal of experience.

How Amphibians Reproduce

Sex characteristics:

✔ In most amphibians, the females are larger and heavier.

✔ In male caudates, for example, the cloacal region is swollen.

✔ Many male anurans can be recognized by their darker throat. Others display horny, usually dark-colored nuptial pads on the arms, hands, or fingers.

Spawning behavior: Most caudates seek the water when it is time to spawn. During courtship, the male deposits the sperm in the form of a capsule—the spermatophore—on the bottom of the pond or stream. The female takes it up with her cloaca and soon thereafter deposits the spawn, often several hundred eggs, on aquatic plants.

In many anurans, the male sits astride the female and clasps her with his arms. As the pair swims in the water, the eggs are deposited and fertilized at the same time.

From larva to adult amphibian: After one to four weeks, gill-breathing larvae hatch out of the eggs. These small, spherical creatures with long tails, called tadpoles in the anurans, grow relatively quickly, and after a few weeks begin metamorphosis. During this phase, lungs develop, teeth and digestive tract change, legs grow, and in anurans the tail is resorbed. Once this transformation is complete, most leave the water as full-fledged amphibians to live predominantly on land.

How Reptiles Reproduce

Sex characteristics:

✔ In sexually mature male turtles, the plastron is often concave, the tail is longer and thicker, and the cloaca is usually located farther away from the base of the tail than in the females.

During courtship, the Knight Anole displays his striking throat fan while bobbing his head.

✔ Male lizards are frequently adorned with more or less showy crests and skin flaps on the head, throat, back, or tail. Many are more colorful and larger than the females. Sex-dependent femoral pores are often visible on the underside of the hind legs of male geckos, iguanids, and agamids.

✔ In male snakes, which are usually somewhat smaller than the females, the tail is often thicker at the base and occasionally somewhat longer.

Courtship behavior: During the mating period, you can observe diurnal reptiles courting:

✔ Aquatic turtles are ardent and aggressive suitors. It can become absolutely necessary to separate the sexes for the protection of the females.

✔ Many lizards display their throat fans and bob their heads during courtship, others perform rapid nodding and swinging head movements.

✔ Even snakes exhibit surprising behaviors when it comes to preservation of the species, often with several males pursuing one female.

✔ Male reptiles can become extremely aggressive toward each other during the mating period; therefore, observe closely and separate the combatants if necessary.

Mating: The sex organs of all reptiles are in the cloacal opening located on the belly. Turtles have a penis with a groove for the passage of sperm; lizards and snakes have divided (paired) hemipenes. While male turtles mount the females during mating, male snakes and lizards approach females from the side. The male erects the hemipenis nearest to the female.

Egg laying: Turtles lay hard-shelled eggs; lizards and snakes lay soft-shelled eggs in the substrate. Only a few geckos like the Tokay produce hard-shelled eggs (see photo, page 56)

TIP

Incubation of Spawn and Eggs

Spawn deposited in the aquaterrarium is cared for in a separate small aquarium at the same temperature:

✔ Transfer floating spawn with a net; transfer attached spawn along with the plants into the rearing tank.

✔ Filter intensively and change the water often enough.

Remove the delicate reptile eggs immediately after discovery and transfer them carefully into a commercially available reptile incubator:

✔ First fill a plastic container halfway with dampened vermiculite (pet store).

✔ Place the eggs in it and—except for gecko eggs—cover with a layer of vermiculite about 3/4 inch (2 cm) thick.

✔ Close the container—don't forget the air holes—and put it in the incubator.

✔ The eggs must not be turned.

Raise young reptiles under the same conditions, but separated from the parents.

and may deposit these in crevices in wood or rock. This form of reproduction by means of eggs is called *oviparity*. Turtles are generally oviparous. In live-bearing (viviparous) lizards and snakes, the young hatch from an enclosing membrane. Ovoviviparous lizards and snakes retain eggs until they hatch.

Bearded Dragons are particularly dependent on companionship.

INFORMATION

Organizations
American
Arachnological Society
American Museum of
Natural History
Central Park West at
79th Street
New York, NY 10024

The Chameleon
Information Network
13419 Appalachian Way
San Diego, CA 92129

The International Gecko
Society
P.O. Box 370423
San Diego, CA 92137-
0423

Magazines
*Reptile and Amphibian
Hobbyist*
P.O. Box 427
Neptune, NJ 07753

Reptiles
P.O. Box 7050
Mission Viejo, CA
92690-6050

Books
Bartlett, R. D. and
Patricia Bartlett.
*Terrarium and Cage
Construction and
Care.* Hauppauge, NY:
Barron's Educational
Series, Inc., 1999.

Conant, Roger and
Joseph T. Collins.
*Reptiles and
Amphibians,
Eastern/Central North
America.* New York:
Houghton Mifflin,
1991.

Frye, Fredric L.
*Husbandry, Medicine,
and Surgery in Captive
Reptiles,* 2nd ed.
Malabar, FL: R. E.
Kreiger Publishing Co.,
1991.

Halliday, Tim and Kraig
Adler. *The
Encyclopedia of
Reptiles and
Amphibians.* New
York: Facts on File,
1986.

Marshall, Samuel.
*Tarantulas and Other
Arachnids.* Hauppauge,
NY: Barron's
Educational Series,
Inc., 1996.

Mattison, Chris. *A
Practical Guide to
Exotic Pets.*
Philadelphia, PA:
Running Press, 1994.

Stebbins, Robert C.
*A Field Guide to
Western Reptiles and
Amphibians.* Boston:
Houghton Mifflin Co.,
1985.

Wareham, David C. *The
Reptile and Amphibian
Keeper's Dictionary.*
London: Blandford,
1993.

The Author
Harald Jes was director
of the Cologne
Aquarium at the Zoo
for 26 years and was
instrumental in its
construction and

development. He has
been studying
amphibian and reptile
husbandry for over 40
years and is especially
interested in breeding.
Among his responsi-
bilities, he was also
active as a trainer and
examiner for the
profession of zookeeper
and master zookeeper.

The Illustrator
Johann Brandstetter is a
trained restorer and
painter. Inspired by
expeditions with
biologists to Central
Africa and Asia, he
became a plant and
animal illustrator. For
several years he has
been illustrating books
for well-known
publishers of nature
books.

The Photographers
Anders: inside front
cover, page 17 bottom
left, 37, 41 (small
photo), 57 top right;
Bilder Pur/Arendt/
Schweiger: page 4/5, 57
bottom left; Bilder
Pur/McDonald: page 8,
12, 16 top right, 56 top
left; Bilder Pur/Reinhard:
page 25; Bilder
Pur/Schafer, Hill/Global
Pic: page 56 bottom
left; Bilder Pur/
Steinmetz/Naturbild:
page 33 center left;
Bilder Pur/Wechsler:
page 17 bottom right;
Cramm: page 2/3, 13,
20 bottom right, 33

bottom right, 36, 49,
53, 57 center left;
Dossenbach: front cover
(small photo), 17 top
right, 20 bottom left;
Hoppe: page 61; Kahl:
page 17 center right, 21
bottom left, top right,
24, 29, 41 (large photo),
45, 48, 52, 56 bottom
right; Karbe: page 57
bottom right; König:
page 16 top left,
bottom right, 20 top
left, top right, 21 center
left, 32 (all), 33 top left,
top right, 56 center
right, 64/inside back
cover; Nieuwenhuizen:
page 9, 40, 56 top right,
back cover; Reinhard:
front cover (large
photo), 6/7, 16 bottom
left, 17 top left, 20
center right, 21 top left,
bottom right, 28, 33
bottom left, center
right, 57 top left;
Schaefer: page 44.

Photos: Cover and Inside
Front cover: Tokay
Gecko (large photo) and
White-lipped Tree Frog
(small photo).
Back cover: Striped
Basilisk.
Page 1: Oriental Fire-
bellied Toad.
Page 2/3: Leopard
Gecko.
Page 4/5: Bearded
Dragon.
Page 6/7 Axolotl.
Page 64/65: Leopard
Gecko.

Acknowledgments

The author and publisher thank Mr. Reinhard Hahn, Esq., for legal advice. English translation by Mary Lynch.

All inquiries should be addressed to:
Barron's Educational Series, Inc.
250 Wireless Boulevard
Hauppauge, NY 11788
http://www.barronseduc.com

Library of Congress Catalog Card No. 00-101228

International Standard Book No. 0-7641-1182-5

Printed in Hong Kong

9 8 7 6 5 4 3 2 1

Illustrations: Johann Brandstetter

Important Note

All electrical equipment for a terrarium must be tested and labeled with The Underwriter Laboratory's "UL Listing Mark." Lamps used in wet areas must be splash-proof. Equipment used underwater must be specially suited for this purpose. Whenever working in connection with water, unplug the equipment. If your electric supply is not yet protected with a central ground-fault circuit interrupter (GFCI), it is advisable to obtain a portable GFCI. When handling terrarium animals and live prey, pay strict attention to hygiene. After touching animals and plants, wash your hands thoroughly, immediately rinse off any water that has splashed in your face, and instruct children appropriately. When working with rocks, wear protective goggles and work gloves. Since their venomous bite is extremely painful and can trigger a very serious shock reaction in allergic individuals, tarantulas must be housed so that no unauthorized persons have access to them. In case of injury, consult a doctor.

1 Why do amphibians feel slippery?

The secretion of their skin glands keeps them from drying out and thus takes the place of the protection provided by cornified skin.

2 Can nocturnal animals be observed only at night?

With the help of a timer, you can control the activity periods in such a way that the animals can also be observed in the evening hours.

3 How much time does routine care require?

For amphibians and reptiles you should allow an average of four hours per week per animal; for tarantulas, half an hour per animal.

4 How big do tarantulas become?

About as large as a dinner plate. The leg span in the larger specimens measures more than 12 inches (30 cm).

5 Are tarantula bites dangerous?

The venom is only powerful enough to kill small prey animals such as mice. But, the bite is very painful and involves the risk of blood poisoning for humans.

The expert answers the 10 most frequent questions about keeping terrarium animals.